# Narrow Spaces
# Fields of Grace

## Tracie Rae Barnes

# Narrow Spaces
## Fields of Grace

by Tracie Barnes

Narrow Spaces: Fields of Grace
Copyright © 2025 by Tracie Barnes
All rights reserved.
Printed in the United States of America.

ISBN: 979-8-9873028-4-2

Published by Altamont Media Publishing
Laurens, South Carolina
www.AltamontMedia.net

This Special Edition
Printed by Amazon KDP
www.kdp.Amazon.com

| | |
|---|---|
| Titles: | Kirimomi Swash |
| | *Kirimomi Swash Italic* |
| Body Text: | Futura |
| Cover Art: | Untitled — Finch Ward |
| Section Art: | Tracie Rae Barnes |

# Dedication

I dedicate this book foremost to God and His healing hand.
I am reminded of His faithfulness to me in these hard times.
I would not be here if it weren't for him.

Secondly, I dedicate this book to Ronnie, my brother.
He has made this possible and gave me the encouragement I needed to get this work together.

I also dedicate this book to Cathy Wooten, who has been a friend of healing and spiritual growth. This work was also made possible because of this wonderful woman of God!

Grace, my twin, has given me reason to write and tell my story.
I have been motivated by her excitement for my story.

I give a shout-out to Pam, low-key!
She is a great cheerleader of my writing. Thanks Pammers.

Finally, I dedicate this book to my family.
This book wouldn't be possible without that history.

# Disclaimer

A book of poetry from the depths of my scarred soul.
This work of poetry.
Making way for a new healed mindset: heaven engaged, spirit engaged, and "real healing" engaged.
This work embraces the hard times and the beauty that rises from it.
Let the words soak in but do not engage in a way that affirms the bad.

# A Prayer

My Lord, I seek Your face in my closet, holy ground, that I may hug Your face, feel Your grace, and set my pace toward a life that pleases You and lift my praise that You may fortify my faith. To a God who loves, in my former condition, a black soul, to the point, now, my soul is white, pure, that You would become the ransom to my gain.

May Your mercy and grace continue to reign in my life that, now, depends on You.

I am frail, fragile, but I am finally free! That I may be imbued with the Miracle of life. Yet not a soul! But the Spirit, Holy and Divine! The God of creation seeks to watch my growth, and I give my soul to You, Most Divine!

Your mercy, so undeserved, brings hope.
Hope of an eternity with You.
Hope of a life that can never be skewed, nor tampered with any longer by the enemy of my soul, because that enemy, defeated already, no longer shouts at me. He is a lull!
And soon to be no more!

As You, my Lord, know, I have opened the door to let You in to dine with me. In a closet, which begets this right to be free!
A sweet, sweet sound in Your ear!

## Part One: A Tomorrow for Every Part of Me

| | |
|---|---|
| There Is a Tomorrow for Every Part of Me | 1 |
| Creation: Divinity Expressed | 2 |
| Carefree | 3 |
| Yet Life Pummels | 4 |
| Tears in Perpetuity | 5 |
| The Night of Dead | 6 |
| The Comfort that Kills | 7 |
| Vigilance Heightened | 8 |
| Just Lie Dead (Not My End) | 9 |
| Rest Eternal | 10 |
| The Price I Won't Be Made to Pay | 11 |
| Depression, a Lie | 12 |
| Reenactment | 13 |
| Words Matter and the Word Matters | 14 |
| Abandonment | 15 |
| The Birth of a Human | 16 |

## Part Two: Sin and Struggle

| | |
|---|---|
| Vomit Angels | 19 |
| Past Follies | 22 |
| Hell Part One: Hell | 23 |
| Hell Part Two: Heaven | 24 |
| Struggle, Gethsemane to Victory | 25 |
| Plight to Sight | 27 |
| Hellish | 28 |
| What Have I Done? Just as Everyone | 29 |

| | |
|---|---|
| How Many Are There? | 30 |
| Narrow Praises to My King | 31 |
| History Seeks My Soul | 32 |
| Steal, Kill, Destroy | 33 |
| The Truth is a Lie | 34 |
| The Comfort that Wills | 35 |
| Glasshouse | 37 |
| Story of a Tortured Woman | 38 |
| The Struggle Still Rages On, But God | 39 |

## Part Three: Freedom in Christ

| | |
|---|---|
| A Psalm of Grief and Victory | 43 |
| Eternity is Our End | 45 |
| Reminiscent of the Pain | 46 |
| Bonded to Freedom | 48 |
| The Comfort that Heals | 49 |
| Submission to the King | 51 |
| Victory in Jesus | 53 |
| Praising for Peace | 55 |
| Psalm of Rescue from Grief Imbued | 56 |
| Fruit from His Design | 57 |
| All Dispersed | 59 |
| Care and Caution | 60 |
| Conversation with God | 61 |
| **Heaven** | **63** |
| Untitled Shorts | 69 |

# Part One: A Tomorrow for Every Part of Me

# There Is a Tomorrow for Every Part of Me

A life of contention fell to the suspension of emotions and tension.

A part of me is child-like, giving way to the child inside.
There are parts that come to my rescue, who love to protect
And keep the shame that ever renews.

In light of the parts that will cling to God
I find myself part of a well-laid out façade.
One that is protective and rescuing my psyche.
It is a right for the "singular" me.

I feel the separation less and less each day
And find that separation allayed.

The tomorrow will be enlightened by each and every part.
A tomorrow that won't separate and keep my mind apart.
In keeping true to my character, I find an integration vital.

There is a tomorrow for every part of me
That rings true to a singular me
Which will forever be my identity
And live for every part of me.

# Creation: Divinity Expressed

The beauty of this world is divine.
Did the Almighty create in 6 days in time?
Of course, by His power!
His breath can breathe!
And He sends His love for those in need!

So, create in me a heart that breathes.
A heart that cannot help but sing.
To love and cherish all who believe
Is Your desire and my present need.

Let life become my only need.
A life in You that seeks to please.
Create a love in those who read
This poem with transparency.

Fruit of the Spirit, produced in me
Will forever be devoid of greed.
For life is grown from just one seed.
Creation from the Divine, all we need!

Forever will my heart skip a beat
When thinking of Your glorious deed!
Died for this reader and for me
To give us a soul forever freed!

# Carefree

Is this life a life that I cherish?
Or by my own hands, will I one day perish?
Longing to press on, my sanity's often gone.
I find myself wracked by my troubles, so stacked.

It's not easy for me to say, "I will live another day."
The easier thing to do? End it all — embrace death's pursuit.

And what if I bargain, today, to remain?
Will tomorrow not start again?
Then how will I feel?
A failure to stay true to what is real.
Chomping at my bit. (Think about it!)

God has shown me new light in life.
The troubles of my past will forever find their night.
A life that is happy, joyful, and carefree.
That is what I desire my life to be.

And there is a tomorrow for every part of me.
Every part will find itself sinless and free.

Sinless, not dead.
Free, life instead.

# Yet Life Pummels

Direct attack, inevitable.
Deflect, react, unquestionable.

Civil war in my mind.
Civility, more than denied.

Peace, removed from sight.
Peace, eluded my side.

Given grace, abundant.
Living in a race, already won.

Yet life pummels.
Bet your bottom dollar, troubles.

Give me liberty, or give me death!

# Tears in Perpetuity

A numbness that never fears.
Light no longer overwhelms darkness.
The dark repeats its lies.
A pain so deep it hurts to breath.
A fallacy so true it kills the mind and body too.

May You strike me dead now
So I will no longer hang my brow.
Please God, you're my last chance of survival.

I need the comfort.
I need the hope of Jesus and His life in all.
Of his pain that turned to joy.
And His torture that turned into glory.

# The Night of Dead

The pain in my head, constant.
And it says that I'm dead.
And its torture scares the hell out of me.

But is it better this way?
I don't know for sure what to say.

So I will go to bed — as usual — with this nightmare to bring me to my knees, from where I can endure, in prayer.

# The Comfort that Kills

Shame —a day never comes that justice for this act has been allayed.
Shame — it kills the hopes of tomorrow's days.
The killer is shame. The victim is to blame.
The victim is maimed by shame's claim.
What is shame's claim beyond the sounds of blame inflamed?
Enough of this rhyme of flames of blame and shame!

Simply:
This cage! What war upon my soul it has waged!
The loss! I have nailed myself upon this cross!
But now! Will I continue in this drought?
What of love? When will I stand up for myself
And shame, rid myself of?
Shame!
I die everyday that I ask myself for nothing
But the mortification of this indignity!

Complexly:
Let's get into the semantics of this word called shame
In a manner which explains its pain.
Pragmatically, shame is a feeling that derides and divides!
Derision. Division. Contempt and ridicule that separates and disagrees!
Confliction. Disagreement.
A clashing of truth and reality!

Simply, shame is the comfort that kills!

# Vigilance Heightened

My ears perked to the sounds that whelm the air.
I laid still keen to every sound calling my soul to bear.

The burden of screams and laughs
The burden of dreams that do not lapse
Awakened me suddenly, oceaned over
And heart like the dog races that never last.

I'm destined for death and that's all I will say.
Because my life was shortened on that very first day.

# Just Lie Dead (Not My End)

Threats of violence from inside my own head:
"Die now, just lie dead."
"In fact, kill myself in some stark way, maybe I can die today."
"Love not received for decades."
"Life no longer lively, it no longer resonates."

It coats the truth, can't you see?
To the point that I agree, saying, "They lie to me."

So, I cry inside, "It must be true!"
"I am white trash."
"I lie down now to die."

Finally, the chaos stops.
As my life drains from me then stalls.
The culmination of a life shattered by one man.
He never knew this was how it would end.

But it was not my end.
It is not my end.

# Rest Eternal

I feel death coming close, to reap of me no harvest of hope.
I desire the permanency of rest eternal.
The last of this life so fragile, ephemeral.

Give me peace or give me death!
From a life of hell I plead for my rest!

Time too short now to hope for life.
Time only to step toward, and accept this as right.
This right for which I have pled for this night!
Slowly, death creeps in over just a short time.

How close will I get to the edge of this self-induced crime?
In due time, it will all be over.

Look, the death of a brave new soldier!
Fighting for her once-heard voice
These last words shall be her choice
"I have fought for years to understand, but now I know this was his plan! Goodbye, now, to my old life!"

# The Price I Won't Be Made to Pay

My spirit is crushed for a lie
and the truth crushes me too.

I just want to die.

I hate the pain, it aims to kill.
But somehow I'm left to pay its bill.

And it's a price that I cannot afford.

Find me once again, my God!
Pay that price for me, my Lord.

# Depression, A Lie

What will cause me to end this guise
That depression is not easily disarmed?

Did God place me here with anger dripping from His alarm?
My anger slightly skewed by my own warpment and disillusionment, yet God's anger: toward the devil, to his own contentment.

To hurt a child of God, with this exhilarating façade:
"Depression is for enlightenment, and it tends to open your eyes to life, relentless."

The rebuttal is ingenious though, "God's creation, never persistent of despondency, that God has sown."

Truth!
Rebuttal of ingenious perfection!
No matter the devil's intention!

# Reenactment

Nightly, I experience the past.
I had ever found that he was an evil spirit.
Ever known as the powers of the air.

The realization, now, is these events were flashbacks for decades.
These flashbacks stopped, and I can no longer fear it.
Because of this epiphany, my mind, it no longer raids.

But when shall the moment of freedom come?
I don't know, yet there is now a sense of hope
For me in this time of restoration and love.

I have so much support and I have lots to report.
There is still anger. There is still shame.
And there is a wrangler inside me that reigns.

I am a powerhouse! With lungs bigger than the sky!
I love deeply and strongly because I have been hurt to my core!
My fear was pushed wrongly upon me, which hindered me to soar!

But I am a powerhouse! With lungs bigger than the sky!

# Words Matter and the Word Matters

How your words hurt my soul, yet not only me.
Did you know?

These words of hate, they send a ripple through society that is hard to abate.

Give me any sweet word and I will skip and twirl, but hate, crush it with every word that we have and can train on the evildoer of this day.

We will find with the WORD
A word that we Christians can relate.
A word that will show our spiritual state.

The shores on the beach, a sandy, watery beach: the words of man can be swept away like the sand by the water that will beat
And turned into a scam that the evildoer will forever reap.

Give me a word that can give life and love to all
And present the Word to all evildoers who attempt to make others fall.

And the life of Christ will rise,
Never to rip away to sea with the tides.

He is always on the beach for all to see.
AND forever changing lives with His grand deed!

# Abandonment

I have been slapped in the face.
Many times my brow hung in disgrace.
I'm not worthy to stay around,
My body hurls to the ground.

When with a screeching halt,
My heart is crushed, bleeds and drops.
Noone cares about my life
Is why I slice my arm with this knife.

You hate me, do you not?
You have slayed me as I curl up and rot!

Just leave me alone!
You hate me! GO HOME!!
I don't want you around!
I hate you! Not another sound!

You don't deserve me!
You hate me and abhor, at least slightly!
I am an albatross in your eyes.
I know I am one you despise.

Just leave me alone now!
As I hang my bruised brow.
Because I would rather be alone
For the sin of me to atone.

I hate you! Leave me alone!
I will kill myself before I come "home."

Home is not a place.
It is a friendship I once had.
It is a place I called safe.
But now it invokes the "sad."

# The Birth of a Human

¹³ For You shaped me, inside and out. You knitted me together in my mother's womb long before I took my first breath.

¹⁴ I will offer You my grateful heart, for I am Your unique creation, filled with wonder and awe. You have approached even the smallest details with excellence; Your works are wonderful; I carry this knowledge deep within my soul.

¹⁵ You see all things; nothing about me was hidden from You
As I took shape in secret, carefully crafted in the heart of the earth before I was born from its womb.

— Psalm 139:13-16<br>The Voice

# Part Two: Sin and Struggle

# Vomit Angels

The tides have turned.
I had fought the fight.
I had run the race.
So close, I was, to the fiery place.

It came to pass
Face down in the grass
On 4th street near the jail.
Devil's minions captured me
In a time when I was frail.

Rewind to the van. Blue Aerostar.
We got the shrooms.
I ate three. In the car.
Way too much for me.
Walked down the street.

Trees were snakes.
People were flopping arms.
I ran in fear to the next car.
I told the driver to get out
Because I had to go to the bar.

Went inside the convenient store.
Asked where to pee.
Stood at the door.
It seemed an eternity.

Then left the store to explore
The downtown scenery.
Threw up projectile style
And laid in it doing angels for a while.

Yet while I spread my arms and legs
Making angels in the vomit.
I felt the pull, an evil realm
And I knew I could not stop it.

Yet as I lay me down to sleep.
I pray the Lord would save my soul.
Grass covered me, got picked up by police
Which I perceived as minions of the one who seeks
Seeks my soul to spite God Almighty.

The power of God brought me from the grass
Into a facility of vagabonds who would ask
"What's your crime darling"
Which I ignored and stopped it before its starting.

Because I knew the type.
"Frequent flyers", they call them.
I knew the path I followed was riddled with sin.
I knew there was a God.
I believed in God.
Yet this road I chose to be trod.
The beloved's safety for me
Had never been for naught.

I called my brother to respond to his invitation
Which in that time I received from the Father, my salvation.
I rose in victory from Anchorage to Greenville City
Where my heart began healing, and Christ Jesus became real.

# Past Follies

In simple terms, I was a hellion
Wrought with anger and rebellion.
I fell to hell, a quick ride down
Blossomed as a sinner in this sinful town.

Yes, Anchorage flew hard into my face.
I became the epitome of a reprobate.
The darkness, so dark, so lost.
The darkness, so dark, it came at a cost.

Times of lies, lies, lies within and without.
Times of drugs, drugs, drugs, in deep, no doubt!
Lies and drugs, what lies before us?
The drugs and lies and lies and drugs, they abhor us!

Promiscuity run rampant.
Prostitution, a run from the past.
Can it be broken by the blood of the Lamb?
These chains will never last.
And in my lameness, I will finally stand!

Because...
He will strike them down with His righteous right hand!
He will perform miracles where the lame will stand!

Finally, I saw the light.
JESUS Christ was in my sight.

# Hell

## Part One: Hell

This hell rages in my head.
I cannot view anything in its stead.
The promise, almost forgotten
Has become something fearful and rotten.

Is my destiny, my fate, stifled
By my adversary, THE adversary?!
Has my mind met its rival?
Distinct and clear, to be wary?

The truth comes out
When there is a gun to your head.
The truth bleeds on the ground
Once that final shot has left you dead!

Yes, I speak of death so haphazardly
But the haphazardness comes, only a cost to me!
Leave me alone, I want to be dead!
Leave my presence while I shoot myself in the head!

Is this real? So surreal!
Is this me? Not one bit of me desires this deed!
But why even venture the thought
When everything I've done has been ransomed, bought?!

My fear of hell, brings me closer to the point of life
Rather than the so foreboding act of pulling the knife.
What hell has brought upon my existence!
What hell will I fight in persistence!

## Part Two: Heaven

This hell is over, no more moments, my mood is sober.
The time has passed, which must live forever in the past.
Heaven peaks through, as to life, and truth provides proof!
Proof of a God who loves me, and the life I had in hell, no more, will scream!

In reality, the life I lived, a life in hell, self-created, yet now is still.
Still. Silent. Removed and no longer. Life is so much better, stronger.
Stronger than before, I say aloud. Stronger than a boar, and loud!
Loud is my voice, after I made the choice to claim victory over the incendiary!

Maybe Hell was once a place I feared, but now the prospect, no longer real.
The life I live, now, is beautiful, and the life I have, now, is bountiful!
Love came down and quelled my fears, which never held my heart to tears.
Still my heart, my life is full. Love, my heart; hell seems a lull.

# Struggle, Gethsemane to Victory

My crying soul, I fail to justify to Thee.
Jesus Christ, the once-for-all-proven Savior of mine.
God, my Father, O King, O Spirit Divine
I cannot be justified to Thee
Without Jesus Christ who died for me.

Your Son, my Father, has taken the nails.
His death has proven His love. He cried
"This chalice, my Father, take from me.
But Your will be done, for all humanity
For such a time as this, I lay down my life to die!"

I have found my life, I die daily for this Man.
To live for Christ, is all that You demand.

Father, I love you, bring me through.
Pain has wrought my weary soul!
May I die to be with You?
This earthly life has taken its toll!

"Not yet," He whispers in a loud silence.
"I have more for you, sweet daughter.
You are privileged, in My presence
I have saved you from the endless slaughter."

So, now I claim my life is His.
He encourages me, above all else.
He is not done with me yet.

I glorify God as sure as Jesus lives
And my journey has already been set
To live for Him, for no one else.

# Plight to Sight

My heart bleeds in catastrophic distress.
Why! My dear Lord, please grant a reprieve, a state of rest.

In fact, Lord, my eternal rest is my request.
Lord, grant that, in my perpetual state of this self-ascribed conquest.
To my beloved, this permanency of my own physical death.

While then, I shall be safe from my feared demise and fate.
I fear the grace of your "beautiful, unintimidating" face.

Because the life I've faced has fallen from your freely given grace.

I will hang my head in this perpetuated disgrace.
I long to dig out of this well called Hell.
But my gaze is not set on the One I formerly loved.

"Please," God, "Father, are you mine still?"
"Please, Father, send Your Spirit like a dove from the Hill."

# Hellish

The anger in me rises up.
Who really cares to hold me up?
Why this constancy of pain in me.
My heart is now a minced piece of meat.

I'm angry because no one cares.
I'm angry, I've been mauled by bears.
This poem isn't perfect, no.
But this life bows to-and-fro.

What hell is this?
I'd be remiss
To lessen the torture
I have seemed to assist.

Torture finds my heartfelt moan
Because of this heart built of stone.
This house, not built of brick and mortar.
This heart built of rock alone.

Tightened by chains
Of sins and stains.
Sin builds, more and more.
I stand outside as it pours and rains.
Peace. I need peace. Fall on my knees and plead for God's Son
to at least fill my heart with peace.

# What Have I Done? Just as Everyone

Just finding time to fall my head
In sight of wine, called to dead.

If ever I would fly, fall down, down
Could ever I, to be called to sound, "another round!"

A round, my death, to seek my freedom.
I, now extreme, in debt, I seek Him.

I love, I find, my God, I sound off
In my mind, my God, aloft.

Will my soul ever be right with God?
Will I have sold, sold it for naught?

With all I have, shall I not fall?
Fall to him who seeks to maul?

God, my God, I seek your face.
Saul and Lot, once a disgrace.
But in His mercy, fall, their face
To speak of His unfailing grace.

# How Many Are There?

There are two of me.
One who truth exudes.
The other who lies and impugns.
There are parts 6 I know of.
But truly. To the one above
There is only one
That keeps to truth like a dove.
Holy Spirit tell me truth
I will shout it to legion inside of me
And never fall for the lies that ensue.

And always find that Christ can set me free.

# Narrow Praises to My King

Tried walking today, stepping toward a narrow way.
Curiosity piqued high with thoughts of this certain day.

The cross, born of prolonged and certain sin and pain.
Jesus died there on that cross, He was slain!

A perfect man, He from sleep, would raise.
This narrow way I spoke of that certain day
It will forever be my saving grace.

I did not know how true, this statement made
Until I found myself walking this narrow way.

In the end, all my desire, to bow before the King and praise!
Because I walked that narrow way.

# History Seeks My Soul

I drank a bottle of rum.
I devoured that demon in the name of fun.
I walked down the street.

100 dollars of coke I would seek.
I met this guy at the corner, gave him 100 for 4 quarters.
Flash forward, as memory would serve.
The forest covered me in leaves and dirt.

Stepping back, I see a cop.
I knew from that moment
I would be caught.

Next day arrives.
No money in pocket.
Hungover and covered in hives
And remembering what happened — accosted.

Lesson learned.
Never would I have yearned
For the drug that could cost me my soul
If it were not for this night of fun, which had left me ever undone.

But NOW
I find myself from fear-that-stung to the Fathers console.
Indeed, I have won!

# Steal, Kill, Destroy

Fear, from the belly he cries in anguish
With thoughts of eternal damnation.

Fear, boils in his belly.
Gnashing of teeth, his reality.

Fear, a construct of himself.
For a moment he laid up his wealth.

Fear, all worth his time. he figured.
But the pit of hell, a time, he repeats like a timber.
Of fire. For all he thought, pride would fall.
He could not surpass the supremacy of the All in All.

# The Truth is a Lie

I believed it once, but not anymore.
I thought it was the truth, but it was a lie.
Was there any deception in my mind?
Not one bit. But it was only truth I had begun to abhor.

But it was a lie? I didn't know!
It was a life of lies that had grown.
For a moment I thought it was true,
But it was a lie all my life that had been obscured.

I was consumed by the truth,
Not by the lies, because I did not know.
But my truth had been wrecked when I finally knew
That the truth I knew was actually a lie
And my life had been riddled with lies self-ascribed!

Truth is something you know!
But when you know it is false,
And you realize it was all a farce,
You begin to feel sick as it deals a blow!

You realize you lied for all these years,
Yet your truth was the truth in your mind,
And a devil you didn't know, in time,
Became the demon, his head did rear!

# The Comfort that Wills

Words! This poem will be full of words I have heard.
It is a clue, what I said. I know this sounds absurd!
Bear with me! I have a message that spurs!

Simply.
Stimulate your senses, with a message of hope!
It is quite injurious to damage this antidote!
Shame was a suspicion which felt so remote!
"Just listen to yourself, Tracie, you sound so simple!"
"That was my intention. It was all intentional!
Hence, simply, you simpleton!
It is not septuagintal!"
This dialogue is the very opposite message meant for this memo!
Onward now!

Complexly.
"The estimation of your usefulness is not in yourself. You have value where you focus your efforts!"
"Perfection is a ruse, in which there is no merit. Perfection is in Jesus the one whom you can never be severed!"
Listen to these truths. Appraisal of these statements will do you justice — persona non grata is no longer your status!
Focus on Jesus' words. You have value in his verse.

"Beautifully and wonderfully made!" It is nothing to be afraid.
"More than a conqueror!" His words will be your master!
"Heir of Christ!" You are highly priced!

"If you confess with your mouth, 'Jesus is Lord,' and believe in your heart that God raised Him from the dead, you will be saved."

See now! The Lord Jesus Christ decided, your soul, He's reclaimed!
"Believe in the Lord Jesus, and you will be saved — you and your household."
This is a story of old, which causes pause in the heart, sevenfold!
The comfort that wills: words of truth from the manuscript that fulfills!

# Glasshouse

I am a glasshouse, forming depressive tears
Or condensation all about.
I find myself fearful of the emotions that I throw
Like stones at the glass walls and brittle troves.

Treasures all around the house.
I fear my strongholds will begin to flesh out
The emotions inside, trapped like rain in a cloud.

Maybe life is not another home made of brick and mortar.
Maybe life is a glasshouse where all my emotions are sorted.

Maybe if I cannot handle the anger
I break through the glass sea of emotions
And crack the fragile foundation
With the weight of my depression.

When will my heartfelt cry shatter this house of mine?
The shriek and shrill created to shake the hills
Have inadvertently crumbled this home
And I still find myself all alone.

No more danger if I have no more glasshouse
That can break with my emotions which spout out.
If it is shattered with a shriek and a shrill
No more will it cause me to fear
A raining down of shards of glass
If I have already been handed my butt.

# Story of a Tortured Woman

I have cried an ocean
And found myself
Led into devotion
With God, whom I have now felt!

For a bludgeoned fool could not see
She is hurt. But a final plea
For her life will cause a woman to see
The grace He has given to believe.
For His mercy, not only indeed as I plead.
But, also, in Word, through the Father's Son, Jesus, I am freed.

His mercy is new every day, at least He says to me
And I bite my tongue and ask this reprieve through His peace
As Jesus Christ, is to me, as my King!

Not only as King, but MY Shepherd
Who loves me no matter my spots and blood-stained record.
He died for me, yet not just me, for her, indeed
That she would be saved and abide in the safety of "finally freed!"

# The Struggle Still Rages On, But God

As often as I have thought
"I have lost my way again"
Through everything I have tried
I have poured out my sorrow for sin.

I have fallen from glory, BUT GOD.
And have taken the long road home.
I have seen His love, but trod
Through the wilderness, there to roam.

This would all be for naught if I
did not learn to love and grow.
It would ne'er be for sin to rot
In this body. Only love's this seed I would sow.

Do you hear that same small lull
Of times past?
And the lifelong role
When God's love be forged to last
Would find our way home
Covered under the blood shed from the past.

Yes! Jesus, His blood ran pure for me, for you.
He found a way to set us free
From a life of sin, corrupted souls, indeed.
But also, for life in the blood, we are released!

# Part Three:
# Freedom in Christ

# A Psalm of Grief and Victory

There is a battle for my soul.
Everyday I look evil in the eye.
Therefore, life falls to an insidious hole.
And I fall for every single lie.

Primarily, I am wiled
By the deceits and attacks of his minions.
My soul begins, a life of lies inside.
The pace of this lie, a downfall shall begin.

"Not by might, not by power
But by My Spirit", says the Lord.
The Word expresses the events that sour
BUT the Word, keeps me from the ward.

Fallen from grace, I fall to my face.
The light must shine through, to my advance.
In my life, the mirror, full of disgrace.

May God save my weary soul.
HE is asking, trust and believe.
The devil follows and trolls.
To my demise, inside I grieve.

Lord, save my soul.. I cannot do it myself.
LORD BE MY SAVIOR, for nothing would please me more
Than to serve you, and marvel at the position from which You fell.

I love you more than life itself.
Please God have grace and mercy on this soul.
I will always have a reason to tell.
I will reveal, to all, who stole my life, and put me out in the cold.

And find myself in freedom again.
To my gain, I shall find, no longer will I sin.
And always will begin
A life praising the God who wins!

# Eternity is Our End

I appreciate the grace and mercy
That the Lord has shown toward me.
Through the church family
Who has been vital for my growth, indeed.

The Lord has blessed this heart of mine!
And shown how He is truly God Divine!

His love embodied in each one of you
Is a testament that will carry me through!

GOD I love you with all my heart!
This finally has revealed in me a new life
I would never depart!

For You are the reason I live!
And I know nothing is more precious to give
As the life of your Son, Jesus Christ!
Days gone by when He finally rose.
Your Son is the one Who died!

Life eternal, with You, my God.
To see Your glory and enjoy You forever.
This fallen earth, nevermore shall I tread!
When before and after, eternally severed!

# Reminiscent of the Pain

As I read the words upon that page
My mind exploded full of rage!

The guilt came next, which filled my heart
With shame for how I had fallen apart.

What came off the page was not a song of praise
But a song that instigated a hurried pace!!

A pace of fear, driven by the enemy of my soul
To draw me near to that place — that pitiful hole!

It is striking, this moment
When upon this heart came a deep fear
To which the devil and his minions drew near.

Confusion riddled my mind
As I endured the progression of time.

I squint my face remembering events of past.
The anger revealed in wrinkles that times surpass and last!

Feeling the pain of yesteryear
In spurts like an undulation of fear coming near.

My last tear has fallen, for woe is I.
I have given too many years to that woeful lie!

I revolt against the devil's wiles
With which I was hand in hand for many miles.

The lie was told, the lie received and believed.
But from now to eternity, I will claim victory!

God has triumphed in my life.
And now, that loving knife is pruning me
By the command of love and away from strife.

# Bonded to Freedom

The joy I have, inexplicable.
The peace I have, inextricable.

The freedom!
The freedom!
O, the Freedom!
Heartsease!

From bondage to chains now broken.
The freedom, no need for worldly things anymore.
No need for tv, cigs, nor attention from others.
The freedom from worry and shame.

Freedom, the freedom to worship and praise.
Worship the Holy One, the Great I AM.
Freedom, freedom to sing, to dance, to make Him known!

Freedom to shout it out!
Jesus is Lord and *He is Lord of my life*!
Freedom, Jesus has freed me!
And that is all I know now, freedom!

# The Comfort that Heals

Providential Christ, I ask you not to deny
The salvation on which I have relied.
Holy Spirit, keep me now, and I will reverently bow.
God my Father, I ask for some form of fathership.
Do not mimic the world, for it shall pass with the wind.

There is a healer I know of who died for my sins
Through the healing spirit of the dove.
The hope I rely on, salvation for my soul.
The comfort that heals to whom all the world kneels
Jesus Christ, His Holy Spirit heals.

In light of the comfort that heals, I respond with a heartfelt cry.
My mind is a battlefield, and there is no reason for another lie.
For my heart will forever be healed, as I am lifted into the sky.

A soul eternally restored and a life no longer of death and dying.
The comfort that heals will always be Jesus
The one who had no qualms about dying.
He died for my sins and regularly I seek the Christ who wins.

He left His throne in Heaven for my sinful heart
For my sins that He knew from the start.
I was conceived in my mother's womb
And He knew who I was before my birth.
He was placed in white robes in a tomb
And He ascended to Heaven from earth.

This is the message of the Comfort that Heals.
This is the message of the God who saves us
From our life of death and dying.
This is the message of the Christ who saved us from ourselves.

This is the message of the Comfort that Heals.

# Submission to the King

This is where we lay it down
All our life to You, this song resounds.
It pleases You and humbles us
For Christ has come with His true love.

We ask for strength, in that believe
That Christ has come to set us free.
He trod through life, a spotless man
And died in pain, this, His plan.

To die is gain, the light remains.
Our life to Christ, we have our stains
But Christ Himself, His Glory reigns.
For He can set us free from pain.

We find ourselves, convicted, remorse
And fall before Forgiveness' door.
We tremble at the King's loud roar.

It seems a precious sound to me.
Humbles this soul
Because of this bloodstained tree.

Humility drives a soul
To triumph in this sinful world.
Like Christ has said
"In Paradise, you will be..."

I bow my head
And commit my life to Thee.

The end will come, a sweet aroma.
Wells of Satisfaction for this tundra.
The life we live, all to Thee
Has power when we set to seed.

Set to seed truth and love
Submit and find communion in God above.

The great promise of our Father!
He will set us free!
Yes, in humility, we will be glorified!

For He has said it in His Word
God embodied on this earth
That relationship with Him at work
Reciprocated to our broken brother
For He sees each person's worth!

Just hold on tight
Victory is yours to have
Do not lose your light
Jesus is the only salve.

# Victory in Jesus

What victory! What a joyful life!
The Lord has rescued me from grief.
He found me in a bind
And I fell straight to my knees
Pleading for His saving grace
And finding all that binds will heal
And in my pain, I saw His face

Give me one more try, I said.
The Lord responded in His lovingkindness.
He laid me down to sleep, to bed.
His love surrounds me in my mess.

I have found victory, and I seek His face.
Unspeakable joy, to touch His face.

LORD God I thank you for this rise to greatness.
Your Word is promise and contract to my life.
Hearing less and less, the promise is at Your behest.
AND I begin with this question, why?

Your word says "I will give you a Helper."
This is why you have lifted me out of despair
This is why you extend mercy and grace to this wretched leper
And give my life meaning, this life you have repaired

A mighty wind that rushes and rages

Will never hinder my steadfast gaze.
Your love is my anchor and finds this place
Where I stand in victory in adoration of your people of faith.

O, to desire the faith that would move a mountain
And part a sea.
The idea that I can do greater things
What an honor to receive
The power of the one who died for me to receive
His ability to proselytize through the power
That came from that tree.

Thank you Lord, You are my desire
I work in Your power and from Your Spirit, fire!!!
Victory has come and I unleash Your plan
On my life, not ducking in the sand
To avoid the past scourge of the night.

Amen.

# Praising for Peace

Soaking music seeks my ear
As I have stayed up for nights in fear.
Gentle words whelming the air
To my Father. Who am I that He would care?

I speak my poems to my Savior above.
I rhyme for Him, because I am in love.

My voice shouts out praise for His peace.
He leans in and listens, as He is well-pleased.

His Word comes forth out of my spirit
AND now I can say, the dark, I no longer fear it.

# Psalm of Rescue from Grief Imbued

Truth, grief in man, anger toward His loving hand.
Truth, anger in the land, while God's hand seeks
To love this vexed, enraged man.

Revived to a victory, unimagined, century after century.
His soul shouts out his God is living
All his joy finds way from misery.
The man's heart once determined Incendiary.

GOD, His love desires expansion
To everyone in His land, shunned.
To find this man, Jesus Christ, His blood enhanced
To cover each and every man.

Grief, sin runs wild, a long weary while.
Grief, His son hangs there, sin, all sin, beguiled.
In man's heart to the one who departs
From his loving start, which to His children He imparts.
A love still present in His essence
Finally, those less-lings are His blessings.

Truth, God loves His creation, devoid his sin, His love embraces.
TRUTH, Savior of this hellish world, the only One to save, what He would call His perfect pearl.

His love has saved this murderous world!
**HIS SAVING GRACE, MAN'S RESCUE FROM HIS SINFUL WHIRL!**

Truth, Jesus, sacrifice, more than sufficient for his life!

# Fruit from His Design

### His Sacrifice

His suffering, not mine, His frame and His design.
But for mankind's sake, I shout His Name, His ear inclined.
The might and power of the Love who died.
He rose again, declared us justified.

His love, so deep.
His body marred by sins that man could not keep.
Lest we die in sin, doomed forever to repeat.
Mankind, sow His Love, endeavor forever to reap
The reward of His sacrifice, His fruit, for you and me.


### Recall, Remember the Fruit

Love of the Father, sweet Love, we need.
Joy, of the Love, pour out Your joy upon me.
Peace, unrecognizable to mankind, we see
That Patience to cause these beautiful feet
To Kindness in every good deed.

Love imparted with joy so deep.
Peace in the storm, obedient to concede.
Patience, through hardship, we persevere, indeed.
Kindness, in the light of Christ's sacrifice, we need.
Goodness declared for men who believe.
Faithfulness produced when we fall to our knees.

Gentleness announced to those in need.
Self-control, bar-none, a virtue to repeat.

Thank You, Holy Spirit, YOU ARE ALL WE NEED!
We are never out of Your ever-present reach!
Praise You, Father, for I love the song You disseminate
To the world, to my family, to those who will lead.

# All Dispersed

The emissaries of the One Who died
All dispersed, in sorrow they cried.

His blood, hemorrhaged; His body, bruised
For the ones who lied, what did they choose?

They chose to deny, deny His Power.
Yet the Power of the Divine would devour
The belly-crawler's mission with no hesitation.

For where is our confidence in our preservation?
Is it in Your visitation?
Or in the "beauty" of the life we've hated!?
Will we continue to react with such substandard stasis?

# Care and Caution

My heart lies low.
In its wariness, I follow with care and caution.
I see the end but find myself stuck in the bend.

My heart lies low.
And with His bread, I energize from exhaustion.
My God, I have rebuked You, and now, me, will you still send?

Will my heart peak high?
Will I follow with care and caution still?
Or will I experience the life that God has set before me
To a glorious end?

Is there a chance I will receive the opportunity
To have a life well-lived?
What glorious day it will be
The day that God will, a life, lend!

# Conversation with God

"No hope for recovery since the inception of time.
Will that God would recover this sinful, transgressing heart of mine."

"Mankind, come to Me, weary souls, and rest will be given to thee.
Heavy-laden hearts, come and you will be set free."

"I am fallen, and my iniquities fight against Your grace.
How I have continued in my sin, a slap in Your face!!"

"You are Mine and My blood was shed for you...
The Great Divine has chosen to walk you through."

"My fear induced by the one who seeks my life.
There is proof, he wants my life, he's tried!"

"My shadow protects you child. I go before you, set your path anew.
I know how much you've cried, just listen to My truth."

"This struggle. I give to You, my Rescue.
You said I have a path that is new.
MY HEART CRIES OUT TO YOU!
Thank you, Lord, for this undying truth.
JESUS YOU CAN SAVE MY SOUL.
YOU, MY LORD, I WANT TO KNOW!"

# Heaven

A large book spans the golden terrain.
My name not lost among the citizens of earth.
He scans the book, walking on each name.
Continues on, changing step-to-step in his search.

Along with the names that consist
Are the names of the citizens of Heaven.
My name is part of that list.
My name, part of the leaven.

The gate! A large pearl hangs off the golden bars, so ornate!

The life I have lived, not perfect but He did say
"Well done, good and faithful servant, you will be with me in paradise this day!"

As I walk down a corridor into halls of gems and honey
I see a man, quite striking-seeming — stunning.

Dark complexion, white robes of pearl.
His hair beams of light, a long blonde swirl.
Hands so big, the One who saves.
Feet so long, they set His gaze.

Bow down before the King of kings.
He sounds like the angels who sing.
His voice, a boom of loud, shooting swords.

Bow down.
He speaks of love with His sweet words.

Power! Power! He speaks with words that do not sour.
Voice! Voice! Sweet with tender words of careful choice.
And Honey! Honey! Terminology laced with sweet aromatic seeds so silky.
More of the Savior a little later.

My stance, awestruck at the intricacies of the room before me.
A powerful image, the cross, the bloodstained tree.

My involution, active and wild.
The perpetuation of awestruck, riled.
No vile sin, no tainted soul, reviled.
Yet the purity of forgiveness, beguiled.

Now, on through the outside doorway
To the perfection of the most striking garden.
The hanging peaches, branches hanging, dripping.
This is where my journey begins.

Would that I could taste the honey-slathered peaches.
That white-robed man traverses the bright green grasses, speechless.
He harvests the fruit as if the most precious loot.
He offers it up, it remains my sup.
Small bites is all I need to stuff my face plenty.
Enjoying the sight, I continue on my route.

A clear-golden track designed by the prominence of a land devoid of wrath.
Wrath found nowhere replaced with love bathed everywhere.
Ruby-topped lampstands, fire-infused to light the path of these stunning lands.
I am struck by the path, the lampstands, the lands.
Astounding!
Astonishing, this pass!

I cannot move on.
I must soak and dowse my countenance with the sun.

I submerge myself here.
I doubt I will ever get to the house He prepared.
Awestruck by the grandeur of Heaven
I am not sure I'll make it to the mirrored, sea-topped crevice.

Maybe I will saturate my senses for a while.
Yes once again beguiled.
I may get there one day, but I'm not worried, because now, I know what it means to be saved.

The man I spoke of earlier
with hand so big and feet so long
His name, Jesus the Christ
For whom I forever longed.

Hell on earth, it was so true.
Now I stand before the Christ, "It's You!"
I longed for this lore, everything I had hope for before.

Yet not just lore, but reality — Heaven, "What a score!"

I am here now, my plight disavowed.
Streams of velvet-like diamonds
Sliding through my fingers
As I dip into the river of beauty and richness.

The struggle is gone.
My story begins now.
My fight, forever my evenfall.

NOW!
PRAISES FOREVER TO MY KING!
HE SAVED ME FROM DEATH'S STRONG STING!
I'M FINALLY A SOUL FOREVER-FREED!

AMEN!

Untitled

Shorts

There was a child, namely Jesus.
He, defiled, in later season
Came to earth, a baby born.
His name, the Savior, beat and scorned.

---

Sleep slumbers tonight.
Activity activates my night
In this time of my restless plight
I find myself aroused to fright.

---

Far from home, I've felt the pain
From the stones, hurled in disgrace.
The love of God, so hard to believe
Yet the road I've trod, I no longer see.

There is no love, in stones below.
The Spirit dove, I only know.

The God of grace, shown on my face
Protected me from earth to heavens grace
from where I was birthed.

---

The park was fun. A daily run.
Jungle gym. Neighborhood gym.
Found a rock. Keep Gatorade in stock.
Played hoolah hoop. Read the news scoop.
A DIFFERENT VIEW. HOW GRAND TO BE YOU!!!

You have just enjoyed an
Altamont Media Publishing
title.

And you too can go
"from dream to done"
with
Altamont Media Publishing.

inquire@altamontmedia.net

compliance